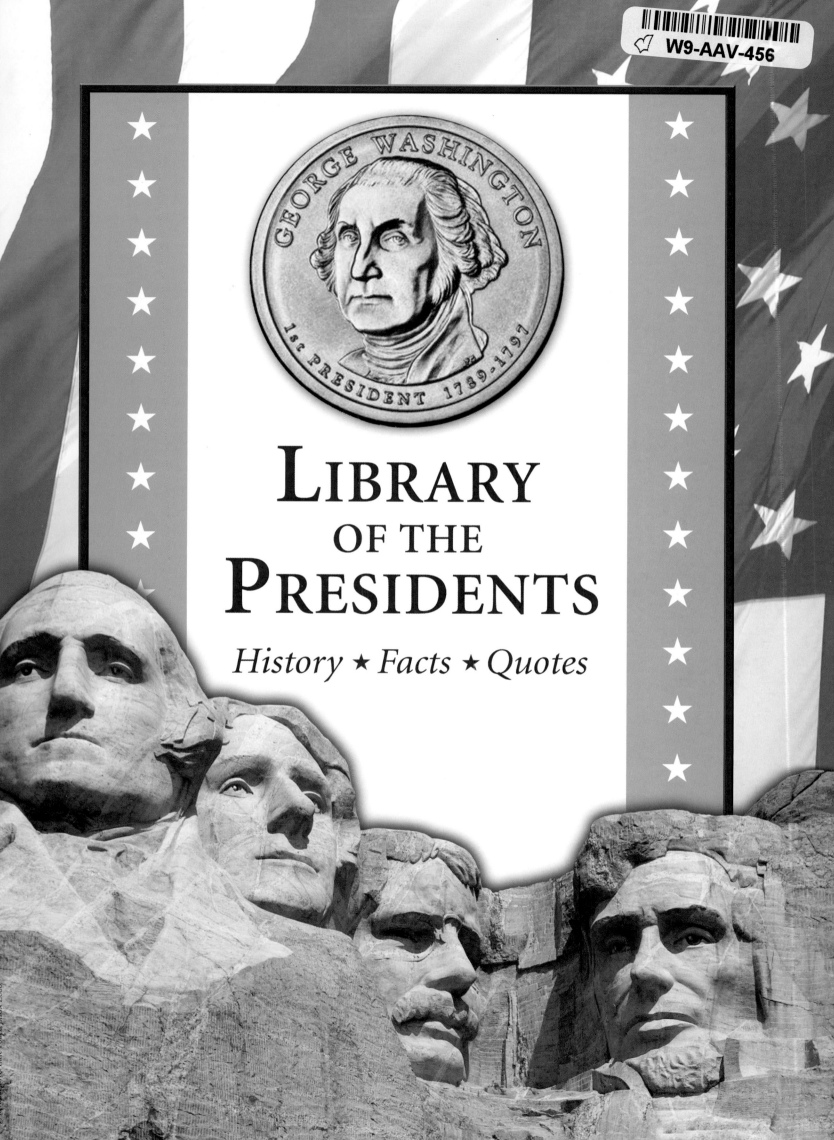

LIBRARY
OF THE
PRESIDENTS

History ★ Facts ★ Quotes

★ CONTENTS ★

★ INTRODUCTION ★

*"I do solemnly swear that I will faithfully execute
the Office of the President of the United States,
and will to the best of my Ability,
preserve, protect and defend
the Constitution of the United States."*

With these simple words, every four years, one person takes on the hardest job in the world—President of the United States of America.

What are the duties? Enforce every federal law of the land. Approve or disapprove every new law the Congress makes. Meet with the leaders of other nations and find ways to get along. Run the largest and most powerful military in history and, if necessary, lead it to war.

To do the job right, you need extraordinary skill at striking deals and making agreements between people who rarely agree on anything. It also helps to be an excellent speech maker, not only to inspire the nation and show it the way, but to get it to follow. One other part of the job: When anything goes wrong, you usually get the blame.

What are the qualifications? On paper, not much. You must be a natural-born U.S. citizen, at least 35 years old, and you must have lived in the United States for at least fourteen years. Other than that, anyone is eligible.

The President of the United States has tremendous power, but that power is not unlimited. The last thing our Founding Fathers wanted was another king. The President, for instance, can only serve two terms and cannot make new laws. Making new laws is Congress's job. And the President cannot decide what a particular law is trying to say—that is the job of the courts.

So, picture a triangle. In the three corners you have President, Congress, and the Courts keeping an eye on each other, neither one letting another get too powerful. This is called a system of checks and balances, and it is tug-of-war, arm wrestling, chess, poker, and staring contest all rolled into one.

No one said being CEO of the USA was easy. As President Eisenhower put it: "No easy problems ever come to the President of the United States. If they are easy to solve, somebody else has solved them."

Over the past 225 years, forty-two men have taken on the challenge. Of those forty-two, nine (including some of the greatest) never went to college; nearly half had never worked in Washington before; nine were born poor in log cabins; others were from very rich families; eight were born subjects of the English king; four were murdered in office; six were attacked and almost killed; and four died on the job of natural causes.

One was never married; one was married in the White House; one had fifteen children and one had only an adopted son. The tallest was six-foot-four, the shortest was five-foot-four. The oldest was 69, the youngest was 42.

All had great hopes. Some did brilliant jobs, some were just so-so. Several were good, and a few—through bumbling, cheating, or overstepping their authority—were downright bad. Two—almost three—were put on trial by the Senate. But a few have been truly great leaders, making our nation bigger, stronger, saving not only the United States, but the world.

"The presidency has made every man who occupied it, no matter how small, bigger than he was," said President Lyndon Johnson, "and no matter how big, not big enough for its demands."

The Presidential Coins may shrink all forty-two of these men down into the same size, but each, in their day, was a bigger-than-life celebrity. The whole world was watching. Not because of their glamour or power, but because they had been put at the controls of one of the greatest experiments in history—the experiment to see if people really can get along without kings and emperors and dictators telling them what to do, if people really can rule themselves with freedom and justice for everyone—the experiment called the United States.

These are the forty-two men who have passed that unfolding experiment on to us.

Let's meet them.

GEORGE WASHINGTON

1ST PRESIDENT 🙞 1789 – 1797

Father of His Country

★ ★ ★

"I can foresee that nothing but the rooting out of slavery can perpetuate the existence of our union."

★ AT A GLANCE ★

BORN

February 22, 1732
Pope's Creek, Virginia

POLITICAL PARTY

Federalist

VICE PRESIDENT

John Adams

FIRST LADY

Martha

STEPCHILDREN

John "Jacky"
and Martha "Patsy"

PETS

Vulcan, Madame Moose,
Sweet Lips, and Searcher,
all hounds

When General George Washington's army defeated the British in the Revolutionary War, some of the officers began talking about the possibility of making Washington king of their new country of America. Washington hated the idea.

When he was elected to be the first president of the United States of America, he won all of the electoral votes. When it came time to swear him into office, however, he was out of money (he spent all of his on the war and hadn't been paid back yet). He had to borrow $100 from a friend to travel from Mount Vernon, his home in northern Virginia, to attend his inauguration ceremony in New York City. He was a few days late—fifty-six to be exact.

At six-foot-two, 200 pounds, Washington was a big man. He wore size 13 boots. He had reddish-blond hair, and his face was scarred from smallpox he got on a trip to the Caribbean when he was a teenager. He also had terrible problems with his teeth. When he took the oath as president, in fact, he had only one tooth left and continually experimented with different kinds of false teeth made from ivory, hippo teeth, lead, and even some of his old teeth recycled. He owned six white horses and had their teeth brushed every morning. (Can you imagine why?)

Washington loved the outdoors, fishing and foxhunting especially. As a young man, he worked as a surveyor, hiking across all kinds of rugged landscapes measuring out large pieces of land. He carried a portable sundial, a kind of pocket watch. He never had any children of his own, but his wife, Martha, had two young children—"Jacky" and "Patsy"—from her first marriage and he raised them as his own. He had two ice-cream makers installed in his home in Virginia. As far as formal schooling went, he never went beyond grammar school and always had trouble spelling. But he did have an IQ of 125. He was a very loud snorer.

Seventeen cities, thirty-one counties, one state, and our nation's capital are named after Washington. He is considered one of our greatest presidents because he saw our nation through one of its most difficult times—its birth.

JOHN ADAMS

2ND PRESIDENT ∾ 1797 – 1801

Atlas of Independence

Born and raised outside of Boston, John Adams graduated from Harvard College in 1755. His great-great-grandparents were among the Pilgrims who landed on Plymouth Rock in 1620. When he was elected president, after serving as Washington's vice president, the nation's capital was still in Philadelphia. When the new capital, including the White House, was ready in Washington, D.C., in 1800, President Adams, traveling with his family, got lost in the woods trying to find their new home. They did manage to move in before the paint was dry.

Once in his new house, Adams wrote: "May none but honest and wise men ever rule under this roof." His wife, Abigail, used to hang the laundry in the East Room to dry. Whenever they had to be apart, President and Mrs. Adams wrote letters to each other (1,100 have been saved), and many of them are very romantic and tender.

In those days, the candidate getting the second most votes became vice president. That's how Thomas Jefferson became Adams's vice president. The two men did not agree on what the brand-new government should be. Adams wanted the government to grow larger and have a big army, and he wanted to raise taxes to pay for it all. Jefferson thought the government should stay small. By the end of Adams's term in office, he and Jefferson were so angry at each other that when Jefferson beat Adams in the election, Adams did not go to his swearing-in ceremony. Years later, however, the ice melted and the two Founding Fathers became friends again and wrote many letters to each other, discussing the direction of the country.

Adams and Jefferson were the only two presidents who signed the Declaration of Independence, which Jefferson wrote. It was basically a letter to King George III of England telling him that America was breaking away from England to form its own country. The letter was dated July 4, 1776. Strangely enough, both John Adams in Boston and Thomas Jefferson in Virginia died within hours of each other on the same day, July 4, 1826, the 50th anniversary of the Declaration of Independence.

★ ★ ★

"I must study politics and war that my sons may have liberty to study mathematics and philosophy."

★ AT A GLANCE ★

BORN

October 30, 1735
Quincy, Massachusetts

POLITICAL PARTY

Federalist

VICE PRESIDENT

Thomas Jefferson

FIRST LADY

Abigail

CHILDREN

Abigail, John Quincy, Susanna, Charles, and Thomas

PETS

Cleopatra, a horse; Juno and Satan, dogs

THOMAS JEFFERSON

3RD PRESIDENT ∞ 1801 – 1809

The Sage of Monticello

★ ★ ★

"Every generation needs a new revolution."

After he was sworn in as president in 1801, Thomas Jefferson walked across the street to a boardinghouse to get some dinner. There were no empty seats, so he waited. When he moved into the White House, he stopped one custom that General Washington had started—the president bowing to visitors. Jefferson began shaking hands instead.

Jefferson did not like stuffiness or fancy clothes. His idea of an enjoyable evening was to have people over to talk about books and ideas. He had a round table made so that everyone sitting at it would feel equal. Sometimes he would wear his slippers to dinner. He hated appearing in public, but once ate a tomato in front of people to prove that the strange, new vegetable was not poisonous.

One of his greatest loves was books. He let his collection of 6,000 volumes become the first Library of Congress. In the White House, Jefferson had a pet mockingbird named Dick. The bird rode on his shoulder and hopped up the stairs next to him when he went up to bed. Jefferson rode his horse for at least two hours nearly every day.

In 1803, he bought the vast territory of Louisiana from France, doubling the size of our country, for a mere $15 million. Then he sent his Virginia neighbor's son, Meriwether Lewis, and Captain William Clark to explore the area and try to find a boat route to the Pacific Ocean. When they returned, they brought Jefferson some huge bears they had captured. Jefferson had them displayed in cages on the White House lawn for everyone to see.

Jefferson liked to invent things. The swivel chair, a letter-copying machine, and the dumbwaiter were just some of his ideas. He played the violin, spoke six languages, and taught himself architecture. You can still visit his home, Monticello, and the nearby University of Virginia, both of which he designed and built. Like his fellow Virginia farmer George Washington, Jefferson owned slaves. And like him, Jefferson realized that the evil of slavery would be one of the biggest problems our nation, as a free people, would have to solve. In 1808 Jefferson banned the import of slaves from Africa.

JAMES MADISON

4TH PRESIDENT ∾ 1809 – 1817

Father of the Constitution

*O*ne of only two presidents (along with Washington) who signed the U.S. Constitution—the set of rules and laws for governing our country—James Madison never thought the Constitution went far enough to protect our individual rights. So, when he became president, he pushed Congress to pass the Bill of Rights (the first ten amendments), which spells out and guarantees things like freedom of speech, freedom of religion, and the right to a trial by jury if some-one's accused of a crime.

And even though the British had surrendered in the Revolution, they hadn't really given up. On the high seas, they kept stealing U.S. ships and cargo, and even kid-napped our sailors and forced them to serve in the British navy. On the frontier, the British were giving weapons to the Indians so they could attack our settlers. By 1812, the United States had had enough and President Madison declared war on England, a kind of second war of independence.

At first, the War of 1812 didn't go too well. We weren't really ready. In fact, the British invaded Washington and even burned the White House. President Madison wasn't home at the time, but luckily his wife, Dolley, was. When she heard the British were coming, she calmly packed up all of her husband's important papers and a famous painting of George Washington, and got away safely.

"The Star-Spangled Banner" is a poem about the British bombarding Baltimore during the War of 1812, which we eventually won.

At five-foot-four and 100 pounds, Madison was the smallest of all the presidents, but he was the first to stop wearing knickers and start wearing long pants. He graduated from the college that would become Princeton. He had a scar on his nose and used to joke that he got it defending his country—actually, it was from frostbite he got riding his horse home from a debate on a cold, cold night. After two terms, he retired to his home in Virginia and helped Thomas Jefferson build the University of Virginia and work on end-ing slavery.

"If men were angels, no government would be necessary."

★ AT A GLANCE ★

BORN
March 16, 1751
Port Conway, Virginia

POLITICAL PARTY
Democratic-Republican

VICE PRESIDENTS
George Clinton;
Elbridge Gerry

FIRST LADY
Dolley

PET
A green parrot
belonging to Mrs. Madison

JAMES MONROE

Era of Good Feelings

★ ★ ★

"Our country may be likened to a new house. We lack many things, but we possess the most precious of all—liberty!"

★ AT A GLANCE ★

BORN

April 28, 1758
Westmoreland County,
Virginia

POLITICAL PARTY

Democratic-Republican

VICE PRESIDENT

Daniel D. Tompkins

FIRST LADY

Elizabeth

CHILDREN

Eliza, James, and Maria

PET

A spaniel belonging to Maria

James Monroe's parents died when he was a teenager, and he was in college at William and Mary in Williamsburg, Virginia, when the Revolutionary War started. He was just 17 when he and a bunch of his classmates raided the British armory at the Governor's Mansion down the street and got away with 200 muskets and 300 swords, which they sneaked to the Virginia militia.

Monroe became an officer in Washington's army when he was only 18 and rose to the rank of major. He was with General Washington when he crossed the Delaware and with him during that dreadful winter at Valley Forge. He was terribly wounded and nearly killed capturing the British cannons at Trenton, New Jersey.

After the war, Monroe joined Thomas Jefferson's law practice and studied to become a lawyer. By the time Monroe ran for president, our young country was enjoying an economic boom. He got every electoral vote—but one, and that delegate said he only voted against Monroe so that George Washington would be the only president ever elected unanimously. The good times did not last, however. In 1819, we had an economic depression. Then a huge argument started about whether or not to let Missouri join the United States as a slave state or as a non-slave state.

Monroe did pressure Spain into selling us Florida. In fact, during his two terms, the number of states in the United States increased from fifteen to twenty-four.

He was probably best known for the Monroe Doctrine, which basically warned European kings and queens to not even think about starting new colonies in either North—or South—America! As far as the Western Hemisphere goes: Stay clear.

Monroe was the first U.S. president to ride in a steam-powered boat, and his daughter was the first bride to be married in the White House.

JOHN QUINCY ADAMS

6TH PRESIDENT ∞ 1825 – 1829

Old Man Eloquent

When he was 8 years old, John Quincy Adams watched the Battle of Bunker Hill from his farm near Boston. At 10 he traveled with his father, John Adams, to Europe and learned to speak French and Dutch. While he was still a teenager, he got a job with the U.S. embassy in Russia. And so by the time he came home and graduated from Harvard, he figured his career would be in international diplomacy.

He was an ambassador under President Washington and under his father, the second president; a U.S. senator under President Jefferson; an ambassador for President Madison; and secretary of state under President Monroe.

Being president of the United States was his least favorite job. He wanted the government to start building lots of bridges and roads so our country could grow and prosper, but he couldn't convince Congress to spend the money. Why? He refused to play party politics, making deals and promises and trades for this and that. He stuck instead to his principles and ended up making lots of enemies.

Adams used to get up at five o'clock every morning, start a fire, read his Bible, and then go for a swim in the Potomac River, leaving his clothes on the shore. One day, a woman journalist, who had been trying forever to get an interview with the president, showed up and snatched the president's clothes. She would only give them back, she called out to him, if he promised to give her an interview. He didn't have much choice.

He liked riding horses, taking long walks, and gardening, and he had the first billiards table installed in the White House.

Since he did not campaign for a second term, he lost re-election. But then he ran for Congress, and that job he loved. He fought hard to force Congress to find a way to solve the problem of slavery. He collapsed and eventually died in his beloved Capitol building.

"If your actions inspire others to dream more, learn more, do more, and become more, you are a leader."

★ AT A GLANCE ★

BORN

July 11, 1767
Braintree (now Quincy),
Massachusetts

POLITICAL PARTIES

Federalist, Democratic-Republican, and Whig

VICE PRESIDENT

John C. Calhoun

FIRST LADY

Louisa

CHILDREN

George Washington, John, Charles, and Louisa

PET

An alligator

ANDREW JACKSON

Old Hickory

★ ★ ★

"Americans are not a perfect people, but we are called to a perfect mission."

★ AT A GLANCE ★

BORN

March 15, 1767
Waxhaw,
North-South Carolina border

POLITICAL PARTY

Democrat

VICE PRESIDENTS

John C. Calhoun;
Martin Van Buren

WIFE

Rachel

CHILD

Andrew Jackson, Jr. (adopted)

PETS

Several horses, including
Sam Patches, his war horse

Andrew Jackson was the first U.S. president who was born in a log cabin. His parents were very poor immigrants from Northern Ireland. Very few of their neighbors in South Carolina could read, so in 1776, when he was just 9 years old, Andrew read the Declaration of Independence out loud for everyone to hear.

When the Revolutionary War broke out, Andrew and his brother joined the militia cavalry in North Carolina. He was only 13, so they made him a messenger. Unfortunately, he was captured and when a mean British officer ordered him to polish his boots, Andrew refused. The officer pulled out his sword and slashed Andrew across the face. He wore the scar proudly for the rest of his life.

In 1806, a man named Charles Dickinson insulted Jackson's wife, so Jackson challenged him to a duel (Jackson fought several in his lifetime). Mr. Dickinson fired and his bullet lodged near Jackson's heart without killing him (doctors never got the bullet out). When Jackson fired, Mr. Dickinson did not survive.

Jackson rejoined the military for the War of 1812 and clobbered the British in the Battle of New Orleans, becoming a two-star general and war hero. When he won the presidential election, he invited way too many of his rowdy friends to the celebration in the White House. The party went on and on and got so out of hand that Jackson had to get a room in a hotel across the street to get some sleep.

His wife, Rachel, had lung and heart trouble. She died three weeks after Jackson won the election. Jackson was criticized for firing his enemies from government jobs and for not always doing what Congress wanted him to do. Critics called him "King Andrew." But one thing he did do was make the office of president stronger than it had ever been before.

MARTIN VAN BUREN

8TH PRESIDENT ∞ 1837 – 1841

The Little Magician

*E*ven though he was the first president born in the United States (all the ones before him were born when America was still a British colony), Martin Van Buren spoke Dutch at home. His father ran a tavern in Kinderhook, New York, in between New York City and the state capital, Albany. People stopping for the night were always talking politics and young Martin got interested. His father couldn't afford to send him to law school, but did get him a job as a clerk in a law office. He taught himself the law and became a lawyer.

Van Buren's wife, Hannah, died when she was only 35, leaving him to raise their four sons on his own. The four boys helped him in his law practice and on the campaign trail when he got into politics.

Van Buren liked the idea of keeping the government small. For that reason, and because he was famous for being good at settling arguments and getting people to agree (why he got the nickname "Little Magician"), he was noticed by Andrew Jackson, who invited him to be his vice president.

Jackson was very popular when he left office and only had to endorse Van Buren to get him elected. But soon the country's economy took a nosedive and his new nickname became "Martin Van Ruin."

The two happiest days of his life, he once said, were the day he became president and the day he left the presidency. He spent the rest of his days fighting against slavery.

By the way, one other nickname Van Buren got was from his hometown. He was called "Old Kinderhook," and that was shortened to an expression we still use today: "O.K."!

"It is easier to do a job right than to explain why you didn't."

★ AT A GLANCE ★

BORN

December 5, 1782
Kinderhook, New York

POLITICAL PARTY

Democrat

VICE PRESIDENT

Richard M. Johnson

WIFE

Hannah

CHILDREN

Abraham, John, Martin, Winfield (died in first year), and Smith

PETS

A pair of tiger cubs

WILLIAM HENRY HARRISON

9TH PRESIDENT ∾ 1841

Old Tippecanoe

★ ★ ★

"The people are the best guardians of their own rights."

★ AT A GLANCE ★

BORN

February 9, 1773
Charles City County, Virginia

POLITICAL PARTY

Whig

VICE PRESIDENT

John Tyler

FIRST LADY

Anna

CHILDREN

Elizabeth, John, Lucy, William,
John, Benjamin, Mary,
Carter, Anna, and James

PETS

A billy goat and cow

Often called a tragic figure, William Henry Harrison studied medicine, but became a soldier. His most famous battle was in 1811 against warriors of the Shawnee nation on the banks of the Tippecanoe River. Neither side really won the battle, but the Shawnee chief, Tecumseh, got so angry at the U.S. soldiers for giving whiskey to his people that—as the legend supposedly goes—he put a curse on our government: Every president elected in a year ending in a zero would die in office.

Harrison was nicknamed for that battle and so when he ran for president, and picked John Tyler as his running mate, their slogan became "Tippecanoe and Tyler Too!" Even though he was from a wealthy, high-brow Virginia background, his campaign managers put the word out that just like Andrew Jackson, Harrison had also been born poor in a log cabin. And unlike Van Buren, who loved fine wine, Harrison preferred cider to champagne. Guided by his strategists, Harrison also avoided talking about any important issues, a campaign tactic that worked and unfortunately has been imitated too much ever since.

Elected in 1840, Harrison was, at 67, the oldest man yet to be elected president, but, tragically, only four of his ten children lived long enough to see him win the presidency. He was inaugurated outside on a bitterly cold day, gave a speech that dragged on for an hour and forty minutes (the longest ever), caught pneumonia, and passed away one month later—the first president to die in office.

JOHN TYLER

10TH PRESIDENT ∞ 1841 – 1845

His Accidency

When President William Henry Harrison died thirty-one days after being sworn into office, his vice president, John Tyler, became the first man to step into the office of president without being elected. Many people argued that he should not have all the powers of an elected president. They called him "His Accidency." Harrison's cabinet thought that they should run the country. But Tyler pushed to make sure he took full control of the job.

Tyler had already served his home state of Virginia as governor, U.S. congressman, and U.S. senator. He was popular in the southern states because he believed that states should have more say about how they ran themselves. His stubbornness helped draw the lines that would later erupt into the Civil War. He helped Texas join the United States—as a slave state.

★ ★ ★

"Wealth can only be accumulated by the earnings of industry and the savings of frugality."

Tyler was the first president to become a widower while in office, and the first to remarry. His second wife, Julia, was thirty years his younger. She started the tradition of playing "Hail to the Chief" every time the president entered an official function. With his two wives, Tyler was father to fifteen children, the most of any U.S. president.

Just before the Civil War broke out, Tyler, broke, retired, and back at his farm in Virginia, tried to negotiate a peace treaty. But President Lincoln rejected all of his ideas. Tyler sided with the Confederacy and was elected to the Confederacy's Congress. He died a year later.

★ AT A GLANCE ★

BORN

March 29, 1790
Charles City County, Virginia

POLITICAL PARTY

Democrat and Whig

FIRST LADIES

Letitia and Julia

CHILDREN

Mary, Robert, John, Letitia, Elizabeth, Anne, Alice, Tazewell, David, John, Julia, Lachlan, Lyon, Robert, and Pearl

PETS

Le Beau, a greyhound;
The General, a horse

JAMES K. POLK

11TH PRESIDENT ∞ 1845 – 1849

Young Hickory

★ ★ ★

"No president who performs his duties faithfully and conscientiously can have any leisure."

★ AT A GLANCE ★

BORN

November 2, 1795
Mecklenburg County,
North Carolina

POLITICAL PARTY

Democrat

VICE PRESIDENT

George M. Dallas

FIRST LADY

Sarah

PETS

Horses

James Polk believed that our country was destined to expand to the shores of the Pacific Ocean. This belief was called "Manifest Destiny." As Polk told Congress, "The people of this continent alone have the right to decide their own destiny."

Of course, this thinking caused problems. First with the British, who were still settling Canada: An argument broke out over where the U.S. borders were in the Pacific Northwest. As if playing a poker game, Polk started the slogan "54-40 or Fight!" meaning the latitude on the map that would be the border. It would have extended the United States way up into what today is Canada. When the British agreed to the more southerly 49th parallel, Polk was pleased.

Then on the southern border problems started with Mexico over Texas. The Mexican War broke out and was never a fair fight. When it was over, the United States had not only secured Texas, but also the lands that would become parts of Arizona, California, Colorado, Nevada, New Mexico, Utah, and Wyoming. Polk did pay the Mexican government $15 million as compensation.

A longtime family friend of Andrew Jackson (known as "Old Hickory"), Polk came to Washington with the nickname "Young Hickory." His wife, Sarah, was strictly religious and allowed no drinking or dancing in the White House.

When he ran for president, Polk promised he would only serve one term and not try to get re-elected. He kept that promise. Polk left the country two-thirds larger than when he took office. Sure, critics say, but he might have done it more peacefully. The job exhausted him and only months after retiring to his home in Tennessee, he died from cholera. His wife lived another forty-two years and would take neither side in the coming Civil War.

ZACHARY TAYLOR

12TH PRESIDENT ∽ 1849 – 1850

Old Rough and Ready

A hero of the Mexican-American War (in the Battle of Buena Vista, his army of 6,000 defeated a Mexican force of 20,000), General Zachary Taylor was one of the most popular men in the country, but had no experience in politics. In fact, he had never even voted in an election because he saw himself as a professional soldier, and soldiers, he believed, should not take sides in politics. He was called "Old Rough and Ready" because he used to share the hardships of war with his men and he dressed rather sloppily, wearing old farm clothes and a straw hat into battle.

When the Whig Party picked him to run for president, he didn't think he was qualified, but he accepted because he felt it was his duty. He stepped right into the raging national argument over slavery: Should the new states of California, New Mexico, and Utah be admitted to the United States as slave states or "free" states? When Taylor, who owned 100 slaves himself, said that the new states should be allowed to decide for themselves, both sides got mad at him.

The northern states wanted him to stop the spread of slavery. The southern states thought new non-slave states would make them less powerful, and they threatened to break away from the United States. Taylor warned them if they tried, he himself would lead the U.S. army against them.

Just sixteen months after becoming president, Taylor was at a Fourth of July ceremony laying the cornerstone of the Washington Monument. He collapsed from heat stroke after drinking a pitcher of water and slipped into a coma. He died five days later with symptoms of cholera. More than 100,000 people lined the parade route to pay tribute to their hero.

Doctors thought Taylor got cholera from the water, or from some buttermilk and cherries he snacked on. But was he poisoned by his enemies? For years historians discussed it and finally, in 1991, his body was dug up and tested by forensic scientists. Traces of arsenic were found, but no more than are normal in anyone.

"For more than half a century, during which kingdoms and empires have fallen, this Union has stood unshaken."

★ AT A GLANCE ★

BORN
November 24, 1784
Near Barboursville, Virginia

POLITICAL PARTY
Whig

VICE PRESIDENT
Millard Fillmore

FIRST LADY
Margaret

CHILDREN
Ann, Sarah, Octavia, Margaret, Mary, and Richard

PET
Old Whitey, a horse

MILLARD FILLMORE

13TH PRESIDENT ∽ 1850 – 1853

Last of the Whigs

★ ★ ★

*"May God save the country,
for it is evident
that the people will not."*

★ AT A GLANCE ★

BORN

January 7, 1800
Summerhill, New York

POLITICAL PARTY

Whig

FIRST LADY

Abigail

CHILDREN

Millard and Mary

PETS

Founded Buffalo chapter of
ASPCA

Millard Fillmore became the second vice president to be promoted to president on the sudden death of a serving president.

Born poor in a log cabin on a farm near Ithaca, New York, Fillmore had to go to work instead of school to help feed his family. He taught himself to read and devoured every book he could get his hands on. He managed to put himself through six months of grammar school at the age of 17 and fell in love with his teacher, Abigail Powers, who was 19 at the time. They eventually married. A tall, handsome, and polite man, Fillmore later taught school and learned law working as a clerk. He served as a congressman and ran for governor of New York, but lost.

When he became president, the country was coming apart over the issue of slavery. Fillmore tried to hold it together by finding ways to keep both sides happy. He signed the Compromise of 1850, which, among other things, helped slave owners hunt down runaway slaves in northern states. The law enraged everyone who was against slavery and led Harriet Beecher Stowe to write the novel *Uncle Tom's Cabin*, a story about the horrors and injustice of slavery. The book turned many Americans against slavery once and for all.

It also helped lose Fillmore any chance of getting re-elected. One thing Fillmore does get credit for, however, was persuading Japan, who wanted nothing to do with us, to open its ports to U.S. ships and start trading with us. Fillmore and his wife also established the first permanent library at the White House.

FRANKLIN PIERCE

14TH PRESIDENT ∽ 1853 – 1857

Handsome Frank

Franklin Pierce went to college at Bowdoin in Maine and by his second year, he had the worst grades in his class. He made a change, though, and turned himself around, graduating third in a class that included Henry Wadsworth Longfellow and Nathaniel Hawthorne.

At 33, he became one of the youngest U.S. senators ever, but his wife, Jane, who was very strict and religious, hated the party-filled life of Washington, D.C.

She made her husband resign and move back to New England. He joined the army as a private in the Mexican-American War and by the end of the war, he had been promoted to one-star general.

★ ★ ★

"With the Union my best and dearest earthly hopes are entwined."

★ AT A GLANCE ★

BORN
November 23, 1804
Hillsborough (now Hillsboro),
New Hampshire

POLITICAL PARTY
Democrat

VICE PRESIDENT
William R. D. King

FIRST LADY
Jane

CHILDREN
Franklin, Frank Robert,
and Benjamin

Just weeks before he was sworn in as president, his 11-year-old son, Benjamin, was killed in a train accident. The Pierces had already lost two other children. And so the first days and months in the White House were very sad for President and Mrs. Pierce. Many believe his sadness made it hard for him to do a good job as president.

He tried to keep the peace between the North and the South, but he was never a very skilled politician. His biggest mistake was signing the Kansas–Nebraska Act, which set off deadly riots over slavery and seemed to hurry the country closer to the brink of a civil war, or a war a country fights within itself. He tried to buy Cuba, but Spain refused to sell. He did, however, add 29,000 square miles of land along the Mexican border. He was not nominated for a second term.

JAMES BUCHANAN

15TH PRESIDENT ∾ 1857 – 1861

Old Buck

★ ★ ★

"The test of leadership is not to put greatness into humanity, but to elicit it, for the greatness is already there."

★ AT A GLANCE ★

BORN

April 23, 1791
Cove Gap, Pennsylvania

POLITICAL PARTY

Democrat

VICE PRESIDENT

John C. Breckinridge

PETS

Lara, a Newfoundland dog; elephants from the King of Siam; a pair of American bald eagles

James Buchanan tried running for president three times before he finally won it. And it couldn't have been at a worse time.

Two days into his term, the Supreme Court (which was mostly Southern judges) ruled that slaves are the property of their owners, not citizens, so they had no right to sue for their freedom. This so-called Dred Scott Decision ignited fury among Americans, known as abolitionists, who wanted to abolish slavery.

Among them was John Brown, a radical abolitionist who tried to start a slave revolt by stealing weapons at Harper's Ferry, Virginia, and giving them to slaves. Brown was captured and hanged, but his death just made the abolitionists' cause grow stronger.

By the time Buchanan's presidency ended in 1861, eight Southern states had announced that they were leaving the United States and forming a new Confederacy of American States where owning slaves would be legal. Buchanan stood by helplessly as the country tore itself apart. He condemned the states for leaving, but argued that he had no power to stop them.

Buchanan, who never married, hated slavery. He actually bought slaves just to free them. But history blames him for not doing more to prevent the Civil War. On his last day in office, he sent a message to his successor: My dear sir, he wrote, if you are as happy on entering the Presidency as I am on leaving it, then you are a happy man indeed.

The man getting that letter was Abraham Lincoln.

ABRAHAM LINCOLN

16TH PRESIDENT 〜 1861 – 1865

Honest Abe

Growing up on the frontier, and as a self-taught country lawyer and politician, Abraham Lincoln spoke out against slavery his whole life. And, so, when he won the election in 1860, the pro-slavery Southern states saw what was coming. They left the Union and elected their own president, Jefferson Davis.

President Lincoln believed it was treason for the Southern states to quit the United States. He devoted himself to bringing the nation back together.

When Confederate troops fired on the Union's Fort Sumter in South Carolina in April 1861, Lincoln called out

the army and the bloodiest chapter in American history began—The Civil War. More than 600,000 soldiers died over the next four years, but in the end, the Union won and slavery was abolished.

At six-foot-four, Lincoln was the tallest president. He spoke with a high-pitched prairie accent and used words like "thar" and "git." He used to roughhouse and wrestle with his young sons Willie and Tad. And he liked to tell jokes when people would get too gloomy. "We need diversion at the White House," he once said.

Five days after the war ended, Lincoln and his wife went to the theater to see a play. John Wilkes Booth, a famous actor who favored the South, slipped into the theater unnoticed, walked up to the president's booth, and killed him with a pistol. Booth was hunted down and killed.

In his oath of office, Lincoln had promised to "preserve, protect, and defend" the United States. He kept that promise and for it, many people today believe he was our greatest president ever.

"Whenever I hear anyone arguing for slavery, I feel a strong impulse to see it tried on him personally."

★ AT A GLANCE ★

BORN
February 12, 1809
Hodgenville, Kentucky

POLITICAL PARTIES
Whig and Republican

VICE PRESIDENTS
Hannibal Hamlin;
Andrew Johnson

FIRST LADY
Mary

CHILDREN
Robert, Edward, William, and Thomas "Tad"

PETS
Old Bob, Lincoln's horse, who followed his hearse in his funeral; Fido, a yellow mutt

ANDREW JOHNSON

17TH PRESIDENT ∞ 1865 – 1869

The Veto President

★ ★ ★

"The goal to strive for is a poor government but a rich people."

★ AT A GLANCE ★

BORN

December 29, 1808
Raleigh, North Carolina

POLITICAL PARTIES

Democrat and Unionist

FIRST LADY

Eliza

CHILDREN

Martha, Charles, Mary, Robert, and Andrew

PETS

President Johnson left food crumbs out at night for a family of mice living in his walls.

When the Civil War broke out, Andrew Johnson, a senator from Tennessee, was the only Southern senator to stay at his job in Washington and not side with the South. Northerners loved him for it. It's not that he was against slavery, however (he owned slaves himself). He just believed the country should stay united. Lincoln rewarded him by making him vice president for his second term.

But if Lincoln was one of our best presidents, Johnson was one of the worst. Inheriting the huge job of rebuilding the country from the ashes of war, Johnson went right to work making a mess of it. While Congress was on vacation, he started handing out pardons right and left by the thousands. He let the South set up something called "Black Codes," which were just new ways to keep African Americans under white people. Then Johnson started to veto laws Congress passed to protect ex-slaves and even encouraged Southern governors not to cooperate with Congress.

Three years into his term, Congress had had enough and put him on trial, "impeached" him, for illegally firing a government worker. He barely escaped getting kicked out of office by one vote. He left office a bitter man.

His administration is given credit for buying Alaska from Russia for $7 million.

ULYSSES S. GRANT

18TH PRESIDENT ∾ 1869 – 1877

Unconditional Surrender Grant

When the Civil War ended, Ulysses S. Grant was a hero. He had risen to the highest military rank since George Washington. He won the presidency in 1868, thanks to the votes of many freed slaves, but his genius in war did not automatically make him good at the ruthless style of warfare called politics.

Born Hiram Ulysses Grant, he was the son of a leather tanner and never had much interest in leather tanning or school. His father got him into West Point and because of a mix-up when he was signing in, they put his name down as Ulysses Simpson Grant. Grant preferred the name, since it echoed the initials of our country, so he kept the name change. His best subjects were horsemanship and math.

"I have never advocated war except as a means of peace."

Grant fought in the Mexican War alongside his West Point classmate Robert E. Lee and later faced off against Lee in the Civil War. He accepted Lee's sword in surrender at Appomattox to end the Civil War.

As president, Grant was bewildered by the political process in Washington and without realizing it, he let several dishonest men take advantage of his trust. One scandal after another rocked his two terms. Grant said that when he left office, he felt like a kid getting out of school.

Learning that he was dying of cancer, Grant spent his last years writing his memoirs, with the help of Mark Twain. The book came out after he died, was an instant best seller, and made half a million dollars for his surviving family.

★ AT A GLANCE ★

BORN

April 27, 1822
Point Pleasant, Ohio

POLITICAL PARTY

Republican

VICE PRESIDENTS

Schuyler Colfax;
Henry Wilson

FIRST LADY

Julia

CHILDREN

Frederick, Ulysses, Ellen,
and Jesse

PETS

Jeff Davis, Cincinnatus, Egypt,
St. Louis, Julia, Reb, and
Butcher Boy, all horses

RUTHERFORD B. HAYES

19TH PRESIDENT ∾ 1877 – 1881

Dark-Horse President

★ ★ ★

"He serves his party best who serves his country best."

★ AT A GLANCE ★

BORN

October 4, 1822
Delaware, Ohio

POLITICAL PARTY

Republican

VICE PRESIDENT

William Wheeler

FIRST LADY

Lucy

CHILDREN

Birchard, James, Rutherford, Joseph, George, Fanny, Scott, and Manning

PETS

Hector and Nellie, German shepherds; the first Siamese kitten in America

Rutherford Hayes was also a Union general in the Civil War. When he ran for president, he vowed he would only serve one term. That way he could focus on doing a good job and not worry about getting re-elected.

Winning the election, however, caused a scandal. In secret, his party bosses had to make shady deals and rig votes to get him elected. That's how he got the nickname "Rutherfraud."

But once in office he proved to be honest, upstanding, and hardworking. With the nation's wounds from the Civil War still healing, he had the last of the government troops removed from the South. He blocked a law that would have stopped people emigrating from China. He thought it was racist. He believed that education was the best way to prosperity and harmony among a free people.

His wife, Lucy, was the first First Lady to have a college degree. When her husband was a general, she accompanied him to the battle camps and helped care for the wounded and dying. She would not allow any liquor in the White House and for this she earned the nickname "Lemonade Lucy." She played the guitar and had a beautiful singing voice and had people over to make music all the time. Mrs. Hayes started the tradition of the annual Easter Egg Roll on the White House lawn.

Thomas Edison demonstrated his new phonograph for the Hayeses—and they kept him up till three in the morning! Hayes was also the first president to try out a telephone. "An amazing invention," he said. "But who would ever want to use one?"

JAMES A. GARFIELD

20TH PRESIDENT ∞ 1881

Preacher President

Probably the poorest person to ever become president, James Garfield was born in a log cabin and lost his father when he was just a year old. His mother struggled on her own to raise the family.

When he was 17, Garfield worked on canal boats and put himself through school, eventually graduating from Williams College. He became a great teacher, preacher, and scholar. For instance, to amuse people, he could write in Greek with one hand and Latin with the other at the same time.

He was the first president to have his mother present at his swearing-in ceremony. She was a tiny, frail woman, and she moved into the White House and lived with the First Family. Garfield, an ex-Civil War general who was six feet tall, used to personally carry his mother up and down the stairs.

As president, Garfield wanted to end the practice of handing out cushy government jobs as favors. Just four months after Garfield took office, a deranged gunman, who

had been turned down for a job, sneaked up on him in a train station and shot him in the back. The bullet lodged in Garfield's pancreas and doctors could not get it out.

After two-and-a-half months of agonizing operations and infections, Garfield died, becoming the second U.S. president to be felled by an assassin's bullet. The gunman was tried and hanged. Garfield is seen as a martyr to the cause of honest government.

"A brave man is a man who dares to look the Devil in the face and tell him he is a Devil."

★ AT A GLANCE ★

BORN
November 19, 1831
Cuyahoga County, Ohio

POLITICAL PARTY
Republican

VICE PRESIDENT
Chester A. Arthur

FIRST LADY
Lucretia

CHILDREN
Eliza, Harry, James, Mary, Irvin, Abram, and Edward

PET
Veto, a dog

CHESTER A. ARTHUR

21ST PRESIDENT ∾ 1881 – 1885

Elegant Arthur

Chester Arthur was as shocked as anyone that President Garfield's assassin announced "Now Arthur is president!" after he gunned down Garfield.

Arthur never dreamed of becoming president. His biggest job before being vice president was running New York City's custom house, and there he was fired for "encouraging" his employees to contribute money to his political party.

But as president, Arthur surprised everyone by turning over a new leaf and working to make government honest. He turned his back on his old cronies who wanted jobs and instead supported laws that made a level playing field for getting government jobs. He also helped protect people from losing their jobs because of how they vote in political elections and what party they choose to join.

He built up our navy and got people to start thinking about preserving our nation's wildlife and wilderness.

Because he was a very fashionable dresser, he was called "Elegant Arthur." He was said to have more than eighty pairs of trousers and would change clothes several times a day, depending upon what he was doing.

He fiercely protected his personal life. "I may be president of the United States," he once said, "but my private life is nobody's damned business."

★ ★ ★

"Good ballplayers make good citizens."

★ AT A GLANCE ★

BORN
October 5, 1829
Fairfield, Vermont

POLITICAL PARTY
Republican

WIFE
Ellen
(died before her husband
became president)

CHILDREN
William, Chester, and Ellen

FAVORITE FOOD AND WHISKERS
Mutton chops

STEPHEN GROVER CLEVELAND

22ND & 24TH PRESIDENT
1885 – 1889 & 1893 – 1897

Uncle Jumbo

$\mathcal{F}$ive years after the Civil War, Stephen "Big Steve" Grover Cleveland, a hard-working young lawyer, was elected sheriff of Erie County, New York. The job included the role of executioner and he personally pulled the lever to hang two murderers.

At 250-plus pounds, Cleveland was a big, honest man, the kind that was good to have on your side. He would rather go to a saloon, drink with his buddies, and play poker, than enjoy highbrow things like travel, music, and poetry. He loved fishing, and his favorite hunting rifle was nicknamed "Death & Destruction."

As sheriff, he was tireless, fair, and evenhanded, which got noticed. He was asked to run for mayor of Buffalo, won, and before he knew it, he was governor of New York. He took on corrupt, dishonest people in government and exposed them. He became president at the age of 47.

In the White House, he answered the phone himself. He was a president who stood up to Congress. "Backbone!" one man said. "He has so much of it, it makes him stick out in front!" Cleveland hired and fired who he wanted and used his veto power to block Congress 584 times, more vetoes than all of the earlier presidents combined. By doing so, he paved the way for a more powerful presidency for the 20th century, something future presidents would be grateful for.

★ ★ ★

"Honor lies in honest toil."

Cleveland was the only president to be elected to two terms that were not back-to-back. He was the only president to get married in the White House. His bride, Frances or "Frank," was thirty years younger than him, famously pretty, and extremely popular. They were also the first presidential family to have a child born in the White House. The Baby Ruth candy bar was named after their daughter Ruth.

★ AT A GLANCE ★

BORN

March 18, 1837
Caldwell, New Jersey

POLITICAL PARTY

Democrat

VICE PRESIDENTS

Thomas A. Hendricks;
Adlai E. Stevenson

FIRST LADY

Frances "Frank"

CHILDREN

Ruth, Esther, Marion, Richard, and Francis

PETS

Canaries, mockingbirds, and a Japanese poodle

BENJAMIN HARRISON

23RD PRESIDENT ∞ 1889 – 1893

The Human Iceberg

*H*e was named after his great-grandfather who signed the Declaration of Independence. His grandfather, William Henry Harrison, served as president for 30 days before dying in office. Other than that, Benjamin Harrison had few qualifications to be president of the United States.

He preferred books to people. He was so aloof and hard to talk to that people nicknamed him "the human iceberg." One of his rivals, Theodore Roosevelt, called him "a cold-blooded, narrow-minded, prejudiced, obstinate, timid, old psalm-singing Indianapolis politician."

But even though his bumbling with the economy probably helped bring on a depression, he did do some good things. He supported laws to make giant companies play fair, to protect forests, to reach out to the lands of the Pacific, especially Hawaii, and to build a canal through Central America to create a waterway between the Atlantic and Pacific oceans. He also made England and Canada stop killing so many seals in the Bering Sea.

President and Mrs. Harrison had their grandchildren living in the White House with them, and the children were allowed to have all the pets they wanted. They had a goat named Old Whiskers hitched up to a small cart. One day the goat ran off with the kids in the cart and the president himself had to run down Pennsylvania Avenue chasing after them.

He was the first president to have electricity in the White House but after he got a shock, no one wanted to touch the switches and the lights would burn all night. He was also the first president to go to a baseball game (Reds 7, Senators 4; June 6, 1892). Still, when Harrison finished his term, he told his family he felt like he had just been released from prison.

★ ★ ★

"The bud of victory is always in the truth."

★ AT A GLANCE ★

BORN
August 20, 1833
North Bend, Ohio

POLITICAL PARTY
Republican

VICE PRESIDENT
Levi P. Morton

FIRST LADY
Caroline

CHILDREN
Russell, Mary, and Elizabeth

PETS
Dogs and a goat

WILLIAM McKINLEY

25TH PRESIDENT ∽ 1897 – 1901

The Major

*T*he last president to have served in the Civil War and the first ever to ride in an automobile, William McKinley kept his Army rank as his nickname for the rest of his life— "The Major."

When he became president, Cuba was still a Spanish colony, but Cubans desperately wanted their independence. There were many Americans living in Cuba and when riots broke out, McKinley sent the battleship *Maine* to Havana to protect the Americans and their property. Three weeks later, the *Maine* exploded and sank in Havana Harbor. Even though the U.S. navy reported that it was an accident, America declared war on Spain and the Spanish-American War began.

It didn't last long. Within four months, the United States had destroyed the Spanish fleet and taken control of Spain's global empire, including Cuba, Puerto Rico, and, in the Pacific, the Philippines, Guam, and soon added the Sandwich Islands (later renamed Hawaii). America was set to enter the 20th century as a global power.

McKinley picked a new vice president to run with him for his second term—a hero from the war who was now governor of New York, Theodore Roosevelt. McKinley won re-election and was very popular, but unfortunately not with everyone.

Less than a year into his second term, McKinley was shaking hands with a line of people at a fair in Buffalo. All of a sudden, a man with a bandaged hand stepped up and two shots rang out. He had a gun hidden in the bandage! The president took both bullets in the chest and slumped down into the arms of his body guard. He managed to tell his guard not to hurt the gunman, and to be careful how they gave this news to the First Lady, who suffered from delicate health.

One week later, McKinley died from gangrene poisoning and Theodore Roosevelt was sworn-in as twenty-sixth president of the United States.

"War should never be entered upon until every agency of peace has failed."

★ AT A GLANCE ★

BORN

January 29, 1843
Niles, Ohio

POLITICAL PARTY

Republican

VICE PRESIDENTS

Garret A. Hobart;
Theodore Roosevelt

FIRST LADY

Ida

CHILDREN

Katherine and Ida

PETS

Washington Post, a Mexican parrot, who could whistle "Yankee Doodle"

THEODORE ROOSEVELT

26TH PRESIDENT ∞ 1901 – 1909

T.R.

★ ★ ★

"It is no use to preach to [children] if you do not act decently yourself."

Born to a well-to-do New York family, Theodore Roosevelt was a scrawny and sickly asthmatic boy who was picked on at school. With his father's help, he soon discovered the benefits of hard exercise and by the time he was a teenager, he was strong enough to box and wrestle at Harvard College. He graduated, married, and entered politics.

Then tragedy struck. On the same day, in the same house, his wife and his mother both died within hours of each other. Theodore went out to the Western frontier to recover from his grief. He herded cattle, hunted grizzlies, and even chased outlaws.

After two years he returned to New York and married an old childhood sweetheart, Edith, and got back into public service. When the Spanish-American War broke out, Roosevelt put together a hand-picked elite cavalry unit composed of Ivy League football players, New York City policemen and, from out West, cowboys, sheriffs, prospectors, and Native Americans. They were called the Rough Riders. In a daring raid, they took San Juan Hill in Cuba and became heroes.

As president, he filled the job vigorously with his own ideals and vision. He believed that ordinary people should not be cheated by big companies. The first environmentalist president, he set aside nearly 200 million acres for national forests, reserves, and wildlife refuges. (The "Teddy Bear" is named after him.) A believer in equality, he was also the first president to invite an African American, Booker T. Washington, to the White House for dinner.

When he left office, he went on an extended safari in Africa and collected hundreds of specimens for the Smithsonian museums. He was also given the Nobel Peace Prize for helping to stop the war between Russia and Japan.

WILLIAM HOWARD TAFT

27TH PRESIDENT ∞ 1909 – 1913

Big Bill

Young Bill Taft's parents put a lot of pressure on him growing up. His father had been President Grant's attorney general and great things were expected of his son. Some historians suggest that this pressure from his parents had something to do with Taft's extraordinary weight.

By the time he won the presidency, Taft weighed in at about 332 pounds. He had to have a new bathtub installed (he got stuck in the old one and it took six men to pull him out). People joked about his size. That Taft is a real gentleman, said one, he got up on a streetcar and gave his seat to three ladies.

But Taft got good things done. He made big businesses get in line, established the post office system, and set up the income tax system. He was also the first president to have an official automobile, even though he once fell asleep in the backseat during his own parade. He had the White House horse stables converted into a four-car garage.

A great lover of baseball as a boy (big hitter but not a great base runner), Taft established the tradition of presidents throwing out the first pitch to start the season. He was also the first president to play golf, and a lot of his critics thought he should spend more time at his desk and less on the links.

His real dream in life was to be chief justice of the Supreme Court, and that job he would get eight years after leaving the White House. He did very well there.

"It is very difficult for me to understand," said one judge, "how a man who is so good as chief justice could have been so bad as president."

★ ★ ★

"Politics, when I am in it, makes me sick."

★ AT A GLANCE ★

BORN

September 15, 1857
Cincinnati, Ohio

POLITICAL PARTY

Republican

VICE PRESIDENT

James S. Sherman

FIRST LADY

Helen "Nellie"

CHILDREN

Robert, Helen, and Charles

PET

Pauline, the last milk cow
kept at the White House

WOODROW WILSON

28TH PRESIDENT ∞ 1913 – 1921

Professor

★ ★ ★

"I not only use all the brains that I have, but all that I can borrow."

★ **AT A GLANCE** ★

BORN
December 29, 1856
Staunton, Virginia

POLITICAL PARTY
Democrat

VICE PRESIDENT
Thomas R. Marshall

FIRST LADIES
Ellen (died 1914)
and Edith (married 1915)

CHILDREN
Margaret, Jessie, and Eleanor

PET
Old Ike, a ram that chewed
cigars and kept the White
House lawn trimmed

One of Woodrow Wilson's most vivid memories of his boyhood in the South was seeing the great Confederate General Robert E. Lee being paraded by in the custody of Union soldiers.

The son of a minister, Woodrow had a reading disorder and struggled to overcome it. He started off as a lawyer, but got bored, and changed to being a history professor. He ended up head of Princeton University and had a reputation for honesty. Democrats asked him to run for governor of New Jersey, and then for president.

As president, he took on many big issues that affected everyone—child labor, the eight-hour workday, the right to strike, and the right for women to vote. He also created government agencies to take control of the money supply and keep an eye on big business.

When World War I broke out in Europe, President Wilson tried his best to keep America out of it. But when German subs kept threatening our ships, he had no choice. Once in the war, he threw the full might of America at the enemy, hurrying a victory, and at the same time worked around the clock to find a way to get lasting peace out of the sacrifice (10 million soldiers died at a cost of $300 billion). He wanted World War I to be the war that ended war for good.

With that in mind, he suggested the world create an organization where every nation, big and small, would have a seat at the table to talk things out before going to war. But he couldn't get Congress to approve it. Years later, the idea would be reborn as the United Nations.

Many historians today put Woodrow Wilson in the top five of our all-time greatest presidents—along with Washington, Lincoln, and the two Roosevelts.

WARREN HARDING

29TH PRESIDENT ∞ 1921 – 1923

Wobbly Warren

Called by many the worst president we've ever had, Warren Harding worked hard to earn the title. His campaign slogan was "Back to Normalcy," inviting Americans to turn back the clock to the simpler times before World War I—and all the preachy lectures from the high-minded "Professor," Woodrow Wilson.

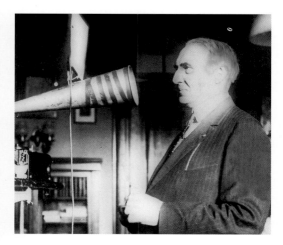

Unfortunately, America took him up on it, and Harding won by a landslide. Once in office, Harding realized he really didn't know what the job of president was. Never a deep thinker, Harding acted as if all he had to do was look and act presidential, avoiding big issues whenever they came up. "I don't know what to do or where to go," he told a friend. "Somewhere there must be a book that talks all about it."

Luckily he had appointed three or four good, solid men to his cabinet, who kept the country from falling apart. Men like Calvin Coolidge, Andrew Mellon, Charles Evans Hughes, and Herbert Hoover. But still, the good-natured and trusting "Wobbly Warren" let a gang of dishonest scoundrels into his administration, and they got busy taking bribes and breaking laws to make themselves rich. The same men Harding would play poker with into the morning hours, drinking liquor (even though alcohol was illegal then), got deeper and deeper into trouble. Harding even lost the White House dishes in a card game.

When the word got out that many of these no-goods were about to be brought to trial, one fled the country, two committed suicide, and Harding, on a trip to Alaska, got sick from what seemed to be food poisoning and died of heart failure in San Francisco. People immediately started to suspect that he had been murdered.

"I'm not fit for this office and never should have been here."

★ AT A GLANCE ★

BORN
November 2, 1865
Blooming Grove, Ohio

POLITICAL PARTY
Republican

VICE PRESIDENT
Calvin Coolidge

FIRST LADY
Florence "Duchess"

STEPCHILD
Marshall Eugene DeWolfe

PETS
Laddie Boy, an Airedale terrier;
Old Boy, an English bulldog;
canaries

CALVIN COOLIDGE

30TH PRESIDENT ∾ 1923 – 1929

Silent Cal

★ ★ ★

"Any man who does not like dogs and want them about, does not deserve to be in the White House."

★ AT A GLANCE ★

BORN

July 4, 1872
Plymouth Notch, Vermont

POLITICAL PARTY

Republican

VICE PRESIDENT

Charles Gates Dawes

FIRST LADY

Grace

CHILDREN

John and Calvin

PETS

Rebecca and Rueben, raccoons; Palo Alto, King Cole, Blackberry, Rough, Ruby, Boston Beans, and many more dogs

$\mathcal{V}$ice President Calvin Coolidge was visiting his father in Vermont when President Harding died in San Francisco. News reached them at night and Coolidge's father, who was a justice of the peace, administered the oath of office to his son, who immediately went back to bed.

A quiet, witty, redheaded New Englander, Coolidge was the kind of calm and wholesome leader the country needed after Harding's escapades. Coolidge's favorite chore growing up was making maple syrup. Once, during a presidential campaign, he asked his father for a penny for some candy. His father told him, No, the Democrat might win the election and then we'll all be poor. When the Democrat lost, he went back to his father to remind him—and he got his penny.

In the White House, the Coolidges had lots of parties. As quiet and reserved as President Coolidge was, his wife, Grace, was talkative and bubbly. She called herself the "national hugger," and she was trained in sign language and lipreading to communicate with the deaf. She was a personal friend of Helen Keiler.

"Silent Cal" was famous for not talking. Once a high-society lady seated next to him said, "You must talk to me, Mr. Coolidge. I made a bet today that I could get more than two words out of you." Coolidge replied: "You lose."

During his terms in office, the country was going through good times, often called the Roaring Twenties. Coolidge's thinking was to leave well enough alone. He gave tax cuts to the rich and did little to help farmers who were going out of business. The stock market got hotter and hotter, worrying many that it was getting too hot and people were risking too much. His answer was that it wasn't the president's job to try to control it.

He slept more than any president, about ten hours a day, including afternoon naps. But many think he was also asleep at the switch and his leave-well-enough-alone approach to being president set the stage for the disaster that was to follow.

HERBERT C. HOOVER

31ST PRESIDENT ～ 1929 – 1933

Chief

When Herbert Hoover was born, his father, the village blacksmith, had such high hopes for him that he marched through town announcing, "We have another General Grant in our house!"

"Bert" Hoover grew up in Iowa, where he learned how to trap rabbits in a cracker box and catch fish with a willow rod, butcher's string, and hooks—ten for a dime. A real-life Native American boy taught him how to make a bow and arrow to put a pigeon in the pot. When he was 6, his father died and his mother died four years later. Orphaned, Bert was separated from his brother and sister and sent to live with an uncle in Oregon.

Hoover went to the new, free college in California, Stanford, and studied geology and mining. Before long, he was a self-made millionaire, traveling the world over. He helped evacuate Americans from Europe before World War I broke out and took charge of food rationing in the United States during the war.

He was very popular when he ran for president and won easily. But a few months later, the stock market crashed and the Great Depression began. Banks had no money, people lost their jobs, and everyone blamed Hoover, who, being the first millionaire president, refused to accept any pay and had his paycheck donated to charity.

None of what he tried to do improved things and by the time his term was ending, 14 million people were without work and many lived in shacks and tent villages in extreme poverty. Hitchhikers held signs that read: "If you don't give me a ride, I'll vote for Hoover."

Although history has judged Hoover as not a good president, he was a great humanitarian. After World War II, he helped get food to the needy corners of war-torn Europe. For twenty-five years, he ran the Boys Clubs of America, because he always had special concern for "the boys of the city streets."

"Children are our most valuable natural resource."

★ AT A GLANCE ★

BORN

August 10, 1874
West Branch, Iowa

POLITICAL PARTY

Republican

VICE PRESIDENT

Charles Curtis

FIRST LADY

Lou

CHILDREN

Herbert and Allan

PETS

Patrick, an Irish wolfhound;
Sonnie and Big Ben, fox terriers;
Yukon, an Eskimo dog;
two alligators that wandered
around the White House

FRANKLIN D. ROOSEVELT

32ND PRESIDENT ∞ 1933 – 1945

FDR

★ ★ ★

*"When you get to the
end of your rope,
tie a knot and hang on."*

★ AT A GLANCE ★

BORN

January 30, 1882
Hyde Park, New York

POLITICAL PARTY

Democrat

VICE PRESIDENTS

John N. Garner; Henry A.
Wallace; Harry S Truman

FIRST LADY

Anna Eleanor

CHILDREN

Anna, James, Elliott, Franklin,
John, and a son who died young

PETS

Fala, the Scottish terrier, and
other dogs

When Franklin Roosevelt became president, millions of Americans were out of work, poor, and homeless. And there was no end in sight to their misery and suffering. In his first speech, FDR gave hope. "This great Nation will endure as it has endured, will revive, and will prosper," he said. "…the only thing we have to fear is fear itself."

He charged into the job, starting many programs that gave people a "new deal" and put them to work. His wife, Eleanor, worked tirelessly to help the poor and inspired many Americans to do the same. After four years, things seemed to be improving, and he won re-election.

In his second term, however, a new war broke out in Europe when Hitler's Nazi Germany invaded Poland. Even though we stayed out of the war at first, our factories got busy making weapons and supplies to help our friends England, France, and others. And more Americans were working.

When the Japanese attacked our ships anchored at Pearl Harbor, Hawaii, we entered World War II and fought it for the next four years. FDR was a true commander in chief, studying battle plans, appointing field commanders and, using the radio to talk to Americans, kept the nation solidly behind the war.

FDR became the only U.S. president to win four straight elections. He was also the only physically disabled president—he contracted polio when he was 39 and learned to get around with braces and crutches, and eventually in a wheelchair. Most people didn't know about his condition.

When FDR died suddenly of a brain hemorrhage, the country was at work again, victory in the Second World War was just around the corner, and the United States had a new place of respect in the world. He died as one of the most beloved, admired, and respected leaders in history.

In 1997, a memorial to him was unveiled on the Mall in our nation's capital. Only three other presidents have been given the same honor—Washington, Jefferson, and Lincoln.

HARRY S TRUMAN

33RD PRESIDENT 〜 1945 – 1953

Give 'Em Hell Harry

Three months after Harry Truman became vice president, he became president. It felt like "the moon, the stars, and all the planets had fallen on me," he said.

President Truman was immediately faced with a decision more awesome than any president had ever faced before. American scientists had created a new weapon—a new kind of bomb—the likes of which the world had never seen. FDR had authorized its secret development, but Truman, and the rest of the world, didn't even know it existed. Its destructive power was terrifying.

If Truman had let the war drag on, we would have had to invade Japan to get them to stop fighting and hundreds of thousands more, on both sides, would have died. If we had used the bomb, Japan would have had to surrender, and all those lives would have been spared. Truman dropped two atomic bombs on Japan and the war came to an end within days.

But the challenges now were to take care of all the soldiers coming home and to help rebuild the world. He also saw that Communism was spreading from the Soviet Union and he put the United States right in its way. It was called the Cold War and it would occupy U.S. presidents for the next thirty years. Truman sent troops to Korea.

Truman was a devoted family man. His daughter, Margaret, was a singer and when a newspaper writer criticized her, President Truman wrote the following note to him: "Someday I hope to meet you. When that happens, you'll need a new nose...."

"The best way to give advice to your children is to find out what they want and then advise them to do it."

★ AT A GLANCE ★

BORN
May 8, 1884
Lamar, Missouri

POLITICAL PARTY
Democrat

VICE PRESIDENT
Alben William Barkley

FIRST LADY
Elizabeth "Bess"

CHILD
Margaret

PETS
Feller, the unwanted dog;
Mike, Margaret's
Irish setter

DWIGHT D. EISENHOWER

34TH PRESIDENT ∾ 1953 – 1961

Ike

★ ★ ★

*"Only Americans
can hurt America."*

★ **AT A GLANCE** ★

BORN
October 14, 1890
Denison, Texas

POLITICAL PARTY
Republican

VICE PRESIDENT
Richard M. Nixon

FIRST LADY
Marie "Mamie"

CHILDREN
Doud Dwight and John

PET
Heidi, a Weimaraner

Growing up with five brothers, "Ike" Eisenhower knew how to fight—and how to make peace.

One of America's greatest military commanders, Five-Star General Dwight D. Eisenhower gave the order to launch Operation Overlord, or D-Day, the start of the freeing of Europe from Nazism during World War II.

When he came home, he was such a popular and beloved hero that President Truman privately suggested to him that they run together in 1948—but with Eisenhower as president and Truman as vice president!

Instead, Eisenhower became president of Columbia University and ran for the White House as a Republican in 1952. Campaign buttons read: "I like Ike!" And a lot of people did. He won in a landslide.

Eisenhower ended the war in Korea but continued to oppose the spread of Communism across the world. He also worked for cooperation between people at home. When riots broke out over African-American schoolchildren being allowed into white schools in Little Rock, Arkansas, Eisenhower sent troops to keep the peace—and escort the children into the schools.

Eisenhower loved fishing and playing cards, but his favorite activity was golf. He had a putting green installed behind the White House so he could practice.

His dog, Heidi, once made a mess in the White House that was so bad she was sent home to Pennsylvania. After a while, however, the president missed her so much he sent a limousine to bring her back.

Ike left office one of the best-liked presidents ever.

JOHN F. KENNEDY

35TH PRESIDENT ∞ 1961 – 1963

Jack

President for only 1,000 days before a gunman ended his young life, Jack Kennedy left one of the most lasting impressions of any president in history. Handsome, charming, with the eloquence of an actor, he inspired a whole generation to take up the challenges of a "New Frontier." The glamour and idealism of his presidency earned him the nickname "Camelot," after King Arthur's mythical court.

Born into a rich family, Kennedy was captain of a small PT (patrol torpedo) boat in the Pacific during World War II. One night, while the boat drifted and the crew slept, a Japanese destroyer rammed the PT boat and the whole crew went into the water. Kennedy led his men on a three-mile swim through shark-infested waters to safety, towing a wounded crewman by holding the strap from his life vest in his teeth.

Kennedy came home a hero and went into politics. After serving in Congress, he became the youngest man ever to run for president, and he won. He asked the world, including our enemies, to never give up on peace. He told Americans to "ask not what your country can do for you— ask what you can do for your country."

He passed a law giving equal rights to minorities and created the Peace Corps, which sent Americans to work for free in poor foreign countries. He promised to put a man on the moon within nine years (it came true). He also started putting troops into a small country in Asia called Vietnam.

In an event that still shocks and saddens the world, President Kennedy was assassinated by lone gunman Lee Harvey Oswald in Dallas on November 22, 1963.

★ ★ ★

"Man is still the most extraordinary computer of all."

★ AT A GLANCE ★

BORN

May 29, 1917
Brookline, Massachusetts

POLITICAL PARTY

Democrat

VICE PRESIDENT

Lyndon B. Johnson

FIRST LADY

Jacqueline "Jackie"

CHILDREN

Caroline, John Jr.,
and Patrick (died in infancy)

PETS

Charlie, a Welsh terrier; Tom Kitten, a cat; Macaroni, Caroline's pony; Zsa Zsa, a rabbit; Sardar, a horse

LYNDON B. JOHNSON

36TH PRESIDENT ∿ 1963 – 1969

LBJ

★ ★ ★

"You aren't learning anything when you're talking."

★ AT A GLANCE ★

BORN
August 27, 1908
Stonewall, Texas

POLITICAL PARTY
Democrat

VICE PRESIDENT
Hubert H. Humphrey

FIRST LADY
Claudia "Lady Bird"

CHILDREN
Lynda Bird and Luci Baines

PETS
Beagles, a collie; Yuki, a stray mutt found in a gas station and adopted

*T*he first president ever sworn into office aboard an airplane, Lyndon Johnson asked the country to honor President Kennedy's memory by continuing the good work he started. We would create "The Great Society," he said. We would end racial hatred, clean up our air and water, and most important of all, declare an all-out "war on poverty."

Johnson, or "LBJ," was a big, no-nonsense Texan who spoke with a drawl and often wore a Stetson cowboy hat. He had a tradition in his family that everyone had to have the same initials: his wife, Claudia, was nicknamed "Lady Bird," and their two daughters were named Lynda Bird and Luci Baines.

He was very good at politics and got many of his Great Society ideas put into law, making him popular and winning him the next election easily.

But the war in Vietnam was growing out of control and dividing Americans against each other. The poor, minorities, and anti-war protesters were fed up with the unfairness of things and were holding demonstrations across the country. Many got violent. It was one of the most turbulent times in our history.

By the time Johnson was up for re-election, there were a half-million U.S. soldiers in Vietnam with casualties rising. We had dropped more bombs there than we had in all of Europe in World War II. And no victory was in sight.

Discouraged and with a heavy heart, Johnson refused to run again and retired to his ranch in Texas. "Lady Bird" Johnson continued to work tirelessly for the poor and to beautify America.

RICHARD M. NIXON

37TH PRESIDENT ∽ 1969 – 1974

Tricky Dick

The son of a grocer, Richard Nixon was the first president to speak with a man on the moon, and the first president to resign from office.

After graduating from Duke Law School, Nixon's rise in politics was like a meteor: congressman in 1946, senator in 1950, vice president in 1952. If it had not been for a few votes in 1960, he would have beaten Kennedy and been the 35th president.

Instead, he ran for governor of California, but lost. Announcing that he was getting out of politics, he said to the press, "You won't have Nixon to kick around anymore, because, gentlemen, this is my last press conference."

It wasn't, of course. Nixon came back and won the presidency in 1968 and was in the White House on July 20, 1969, when astronaut Neil Armstrong put the first human footprints on the moon.

Nixon was very clever when it came to getting votes. Some said too clever and gave him the nickname "Tricky Dick." He got elected president by promising to end the war in Vietnam, but the war dragged on and on.

He brought troops home little by little, but increased the bombing. "Peace is at hand," the White House kept telling everybody. As protests got worse, 20,000 more Americans died before he could finally get U.S. soldiers out of Vietnam completely.

To his credit, Nixon did start talking with the Communist giants China and the Soviet Union, but his "tricks" caught up with him.

Running for re-election in 1972, he was to win by a mile. But, wanting to be sure, his assistants had been spying on the competition. When his spies were caught, most of them lied. So did Nixon. He resigned in disgrace rather than be impeached—get put on trial—by the Senate.

"Always remember," he said, "others may hate you, but those who hate you don't win unless you hate them. And then you destroy yourself."

"I am not a crook."

★ AT A GLANCE ★

BORN

January 9, 1913
Yorba Linda, California

POLITICAL PARTY

Republican

VICE PRESIDENTS

Spiro T. Agnew;
Gerald R. Ford

FIRST LADY

Thelma "Pat"

CHILDREN

Patricia "Tricia" and Julie

PETS

Checkers, a spaniel; Vicky, a poodle; Pasha, a terrier; King Timahoe, an Irish setter

GERALD R. FORD

38TH PRESIDENT ∾ 1974 – 1977

Jerry

Jerry Ford became president when Richard Nixon resigned in disgrace. "My fellow Americans," he said, entering the White House. "Our long national nightmare is over." The dark days of people not trusting their president were over. He made it his goal to restore people's faith.

And he knew something about scoring goals. A star football player, he was an All-American center and linebacker for the Michigan Wolverines and led them to two undefeated, championship seasons. "I had pro offers from the Detroit Lions and Green Bay Packers," he said later. "If I had gone into professional football, the name Jerry Ford might have been a household word today."

Instead he went to Yale Law School and paid his tuition by coaching Yale's JV football team and boxing. He graduated in the top quarter of his class, even though he had been so busy with his coaching duties.

Ford served on an aircraft carrier in the Pacific in World War II and then became a congressman and served for twenty-five years. His biggest hope was to be Speaker of the House, but he had to settle for vice president and then president.

By pardoning Richard Nixon, Ford ruined his chances for continuing as president. Some people thought something fishy was going on. But Ford did it, he said, because it was the right thing to do, to help heal the country.

Ford often said that the thing he was proudest of in his life was making Eagle in the Boy Scouts. He always kept a copy of the Boy Scout manual on his desk throughout his career. When he died in 2006, more than 400 Eagle Scouts formed an honor guard at his state funeral.

His wife, Betty, has worked tirelessly to help people overcome their dependencies on drugs and alcohol.

★ ★ ★

"I am a Ford, not a Lincoln."

★ AT A GLANCE ★

BORN

July 14, 1913
Omaha, Nebraska

POLITICAL PARTY

Republican

FIRST LADY

Elizabeth Anne "Betty"

CHILDREN

Michael, John, Steven, and Susan

PET

Liberty, a golden retriever, who gave birth to a litter of puppies in the White House

JIMMY CARTER

39TH PRESIDENT ∾ 1977 – 1981

Jimbo

Jimmy Carter grew up on his family's peanut farm in Georgia. He studied nuclear physics at the U.S. Naval Academy at Annapolis and worked as an engineer running the engines on a nuclear submarine. When his father died in 1953, Jimmy went home to run the farm and soon got into politics, rising to governor of Georgia.

When he ran for president, people liked him because he was an "outsider" in Washington. Voters were tired of all the wheelers and dealers in the government and wanted someone new who wasn't "connected." Carter was a born-again Christian with very high moral standards.

The problem was, there was a worldwide energy crisis going on—gas prices were skyrocketing out of control. Cars had to wait in long lines just to buy gas. And it got more expensive than ever to borrow money to buy a house.

Overseas in Iran, protesters stormed our embassy and took fifty-two U.S. diplomats hostage and held them as prisoners for 444 days. Carter worked around the clock to get them free, but couldn't.

Not being a Washington "insider" worked against President Carter. He had trouble getting Congress to go along with him on many of his ideas to solve these problems. And things just didn't seem to get any better. He lost re-election.

An extremely intelligent, decent, and sincere man, Carter was the third U.S. president to be awarded the Nobel Peace Prize, in his case, for forging a peace treaty between warring sides in the Middle East.

"War may be a necessary evil," he said. "But no matter how necessary, it is always an evil, never a good. We will not learn to live together in peace by killing each other's children."

After leaving the White House, he and Mrs. Carter worked to build homes for the homeless, often taking up hammer and nails and doing the carpentry themselves.

"Wherever life takes us, there are always moments of wonder."

★ AT A GLANCE ★

BORN

October 1, 1924
Plains, Georgia

POLITICAL PARTY

Democrat

VICE PRESIDENT

Walter Mondale

FIRST LADY

Rosalynn

CHILDREN

John "Jack,"
James Earl III "Chip,"
Jeffrey "Jeff," and Amy

PETS

Grits, a collie; Misty Malarky Ying Yang, a Siamese cat

RONALD REAGAN

40TH PRESIDENT ∞ 1981 – 1989

The Great Communicator

★ ★ ★

"Don't be afraid to see what you see."

★ AT A GLANCE ★

BORN
February 6, 1911
Tampico, Illinois

POLITICAL PARTY
Republican

VICE PRESIDENT
George H. W. Bush

FIRST LADY
Nancy

CHILDREN
Maureen, Michael, Patricia,
and Ronald

PETS
Lucky, a Bouvier des Flandres;
Rex, a King Charles spaniel

At 69, former movie star Ronald Reagan was the oldest president ever to enter the White House. He joked: "Thomas Jefferson once said, 'We should never judge a president by his age, only by his works.' And ever since he told me that, I stopped worrying."

Called the Great Communicator, Reagan was perfectly at ease in front of cameras and large crowds. His years in Hollywood had prepared him for one of the greatest demands of the job: winning people over.

"How can a president not be an actor?" he asked.

His high school teacher used to make him read his papers out loud in front of the class. "Maybe that's where the 'ham' began," he said.

He made more than fifty movies for Warner Brothers Studios, usually cast as the wholesome All-American kid. He was second only to Errol Flynn in amount of fan mail. He then went to work for General Electric as a television host and became familiar to even more Americans.

When he entered politics, he rose quickly, serving as governor of California for eight years. (A job another popular movie actor would one day hold.)

Running for president his message was that government was too big and reducing taxes for the rich would help everyone when their wealth "trickled down" to the less wealthy. Instead of economics, critics called it Reaganomics.

Shortly after he took office, a deranged gunman tried to assassinate him outside of a hotel in Washington, D.C. While doctors got ready to take the bullet out of his lung at the hospital, he joked to Nancy, the First Lady, "Sorry, honey, I forgot to duck."

Reagan will be remembered for hurrying the end of the Cold War and for trying to make the government work better. "I have wondered at times," he said, "what the Ten Commandments would have looked like if Moses had run them through the U.S. Congress."

GEORGE H.W. BUSH

41ST PRESIDENT ∽ 1989 – 1993

Poppy

George Bush put off going to college and joined the military during World War II. He was the youngest pilot in the Navy and flew fifty-eight combat missions in the Pacific. He won the Distinguished Flying Cross for bravery. He came home and graduated with honors from Yale, worked in the oil business, and then got into politics.

By the time Ronald Reagan picked him to run as vice president, Bush had served in several top government jobs, including head of the Central Intelligence Agency, or CIA.

As vice president, he organized all branches of the military to cooperate and try to stop the flow of illegal drugs into our country. Code-named Operation Blue Lightning, it equipped jets, speed boats, and helicopters with state-of-the-art sensors and tracking devices to snag drug smugglers as they tried to land on our shores.

In 1988, George Bush became the first vice president elected to president since Martin Van Buren in 1836.

When Iraq invaded Kuwait, he sent a force into the Persian Gulf and drove back Saddam Hussein's invasion. He was popular for a while, but the sagging economy prevented him from getting re-elected.

As president, he did have a sense of humor. He once said, "I do not like broccoli. And I haven't liked it since I was a little kid and my mother made me eat it. And I'm President of the United States and I'm not going to eat any more broccoli."

His wife, Barbara, became spokesperson for reading and helped write their dog's best-selling book about life in the White House—*Millie's Book.*

★ ★ ★

"We are not the sum of our possessions."

★ AT A GLANCE ★

BORN

June 12, 1924
Milton, Massachusetts

POLITICAL PARTY

Republican

VICE PRESIDENT

J. Danforth ("Dan") Quayle

FIRST LADY

Barbara

CHILDREN

George W., Robin, John Ellis "Jeb," Neil, Marvin, and Dorothy

PET

Millie, a springer spaniel

WILLIAM J. CLINTON

42ND PRESIDENT ∾ 1993 – 2001

Slick Willie

When Bill Clinton was 16, he was an elected delegate to Boys Nation, a youth organization. The group gathered in Washington, D.C. where he met and shook hands with President John F. Kennedy. From then on, he said, Kennedy was his hero and role model.

A bright student, Clinton studied at Oxford University as a Rhodes scholar and graduated from Yale Law School. At the age of 32, he became the governor of Arkansas, the youngest governor in the country. He was elected president fourteen years later.

As president, Clinton gained respect in foreign countries, especially for helping to end conflict in central Europe. And he helped the economy at home. He relaxed by playing the saxophone, playing the card game Hearts, and doing crossword puzzles. He was the first Democratic president elected to a second term since FDR.

But Clinton became only the second president to be impeached—or put on trial—by the Senate for misbehavior in office. Still, he remained a very strong and powerful spokesman for the Democratic Party. His presidential library will be located in Little Rock, Arkansas.

And his wife, Hillary Rodham, went on to make history, becoming the first ever ex-First Lady to run for the U.S. Senate and win, and the first ex-First Lady to announce that she would run for her husband's old job—president of the United States.

Historians and experts are now scratching their heads trying to figure out how they would refer to an ex-president who is now a president's spouse: First Gentleman?

★ ★ ★

"There is nothing wrong with America that cannot be cured by what is right with America."

★ AT A GLANCE ★

BORN
August 19, 1946
Hope, Arkansas

POLITICAL PARTY
Democrat

VICE PRESIDENT
Albert Gore

FIRST LADY
Hillary Rodham

CHILD
Chelsea Victoria

PETS
Socks, a cat; Buddy, a dog

GEORGE W. BUSH

43RD PRESIDENT ∾ 2001 –

W. (Dubya)

The 2000 presidential election was such a close race that it took forty extra days to count all the votes. Finally, the Supreme Court had to decide which of the candidates— Al Gore or George W. Bush—had actually won it. When the high court voted 5-to-4 that Bush was the winner, it was only the second time in history that a former president's son had won the office himself. (John Quincy Adams was the first, 175 years earlier.) George W's father once referred to him affectionately as "my boy Quincy."

Although he was born in Connecticut, he moved as a toddler to Texas and had a happy childhood. Until tragedy struck. His little sister Robin died from childhood leukemia and the whole family was deeply saddened and grew closer than ever.

George "W." went to Yale and then Harvard Business School, after spending a year flying F-102 fighter jets for the Air National Guard.

The governor of Texas, Bush was also, for a while, part owner of the Texas Rangers baseball team. He came to the White House wanting to improve education and lower taxes, but history stepped in and shifted his focus.

On September 11, 2001, terrorists hijacked American airliners and crashed them into the World Trade Center in New York City and into the Pentagon (our nation's military headquarters) near Washington. President Bush declared war on terrorism. He created a new Department of Homeland Security to help make sure attacks like that wouldn't happen again. And he sent our forces to invade Afghanistan, where the terrorists had their headquarters.

He also became convinced that Iraq's brutal dictator, Saddam Hussein, was involved in terrorism and convinced Congress to authorize an invasion of Iraq.

"America was targeted for attack," he said, "because we are the brightest beacon for freedom and opportunity in the world. And no one will keep that light from shining."

"America will never seek a permission slip to defend the security of our people."

★ AT A GLANCE ★

BORN
July 6, 1946
New Haven, Connecticut

POLITICAL PARTY
Republican

VICE PRESIDENT
Richard Cheney

FIRST LADY
Laura

CHILDREN
Barbara and Jenna (twins)

PETS
Miss Beazley and Barney, Scottish terriers; India, a cat

★ COIN RELEASE SCHEDULE ★

PRESIDENT	RELEASE YEAR
1. George Washington	2007
2. John Adams	2007
3. Thomas Jefferson	2007
4. James Madison	2007
5. James Monroe	2008
6. John Quincy Adams	2008
7. Andrew Jackson	2008
8. Martin Van Buren	2008
9. William Henry Harrison	2009
10. John Tyler	2009
11. James K. Polk	2009
12. Zachary Taylor	2009
13. Millard Fillmore	2010
14. Franklin Pierce	2010
15. James Buchanan	2010
16. Abraham Lincoln	2010
17. Andrew Johnson	2011
18. Ulysses S. Grant	2011
19. Rutherford B. Hayes	2011
20. James A. Garfield	2011
21. Chester A. Arthur	2012
22. Stephen Grover Cleveland	2012
23. Benjamin Harrison	2012
24. Stephen Grover Cleveland	2012

PRESIDENT	RELEASE YEAR
25. William McKinley	2013
26. Theodore Roosevelt	2013
27. William Howard Taft	2013
28. Woodrow Wilson	2013
29. Warren Harding	2014
30. Calvin Coolidge	2014
31. Herbert C. Hoover	2014
32. Franklin D. Roosevelt	2014
33. Harry S Truman	2015
34. Dwight D. Eisenhower	2015
35. John F. Kennedy	2015
36. Lyndon B. Johnson	2015
37. Richard M. Nixon	2016
38. Gerald R. Ford	2016
39. Jimmy Carter	*
40. Ronald Reagan	*
41. George H. W. Bush	*
42. William J. Clinton	*
43. George W. Bush	*

*At the time of publication, the release dates for these presidents had not yet been scheduled.